Ollie Maddigan

The Olive Boy

Salamander Street

PLAYS

First published in 2026 by Salamander Street Ltd., a Wordville imprint. (info@salamanderstreet.com).

The Olive Boy © Ollie Maddigan, 2026

Cover photograph by Origin Studio.

ISBN: 9781068233487

10 9 8 7 6 5 4 3 2 1

Further copies of this publication can be purchased from www.salamanderstreet.com

The Olive Boy was first performed at the Hope Theatre in 2021, and later presented at the Edinburgh Fringe in 2022. The production then went on a national tour in 2024 before being staged at Southwark Playhouse Borough in 2025.

We would like to thank and show our gratitude to:
Andrew Wood
Mitch Donaldson
Becky Bartram R
Ray Böhm
Cerys K Baker
Cathy and Amanda
Matthew Maddigan
John McCrea
Brenda Gilhooly
Alison Carvalho
Carl Duffet
Micheal
Ronni Ancona
H

And everyone who has supported the show over the years.

The Olive Boy	**Ollie Maddigan**
The Voice	**Ronni Ancona**
Director	**Scott Le Crass**
Stage Manager	**Dani White**
Lighting Director	**Adam Jeffery**
Producer	**Free Run Productions**
Associate Producer	**Shoddy Theatre**

CREATIVE TEAM

Ollie Maddigan | Writer & Performer

Ollie Maddigan is a writer-performer raised in Oxfordshire and based in London. He trained at The BRIT School before briefly attending drama school, ultimately leaving after two months to focus on creating his own work.

His debut play, *The Olive Boy*—drawn from his experiences of teenage grief and growing up—became a breakthrough project, earning an OFFIE *(Off West End Award)* for Creation. The show has resonated with audiences for its mix of humour, honesty and personal storytelling, and has been praised by figures including Steve Pemberton, who described Ollie as "one to watch."

Ollie continues to make work rooted in real life, exploring adolescence, loss and identity through a voice that is both candid and sharply comedic.

Ronni Ancona | The Voice

Ronni Ancona is a British actress, comedian, writer and impressionist, best known for her work in television comedy and character performance. She rose to prominence with *The Big Impression* and as a core cast member of the BAFTA-winning series *Smack the Pony*. Her extensive screen credits include *Dead Ringers, The Sketch Show, Getting On, Motherland* and *Friday Night Dinner*. Renowned for her sharp observational humour and transformative character work, Ancona has also worked widely in theatre, radio and voice performance, establishing herself as one of the UK's most versatile and respected comedy performers.

Scott Le Crass | Director

Scott was born in Bristol, grew up in Birmingham, trained as an actor at Arts Ed and was a director on the Birmingham Rep's first Foundry Programme. In 2022, he completed the National Theatre Director's Course.

He is an Associate Director for Pleasure Dome Theatre Company and has directed all their productions to date.

Scott directed the Off Com award-winning digital revival of *Rose* by Martin Sherman starring Maureen Lipman (Hope Mill Theatre/Sky Arts/Broadway HD). In 2023 he was nominated for Best Creative West End Debut at The Stage Awards for his production of *Rose*. In 2022, he received an Off West End and Broadway World nomination for Best Director for *Rose*. In 2024 *Rose* won an Off West End award for Best Solo Performance.

Credits include: Director—*Rose* (West End), *Cut The Crap* starring Sharon Osbourne (West End), *Elmer* (UK and International Tour/Sell A Door), *Sid* (Arts Theatre and UK Tour), *Toxic* (HOME, Manchester/UK tour), *Buff* (UK tour), *Nostos* (Southwark Playhouse), *Marshmallow Me* (UK tour), *Second Summer of Love* (UK tour), *The Witches* (Watford Palace), *Alice in Wonderland* (Old, Rep, Birmingham), *Jab* (Finborough Theatre/ Park Theatre), *Rose* (Hope Mill Theatre/Park Theatre), *Country Music* (Omnibus Theatre), *Zanna Don't* (Old Joint Stock Theatre), *Shooting Star, The Musical (*The Two Brewers, Clapham), *The Mad Gay King* (King's Head Theatre), *My Life As A Cowboy* (Omnibus Theatre), *Did You Mean To Fall Like That* (Edinburgh Fringe), *Pillock* (Contact Theatre/Edinburgh Fringe), *Wormholes* (Omnibus Theatre), *The Railway Children* (OVO Roman Theatre), *My Dear Aunty Nell* (Tour), *Merboy* (Omnibus Theatre), *Thirsty* (Vault Festival), *Twelfth Night* (East London Shakespeare Festival), *I Couldn't Do Your Job* (Pleasance Theatre, London/Queens Theatre, Hornchurch), *If You Love Me This Might Hurt* by Matty May (Camden People's Theatre), *Education, Education, Karaoke* (Camden People's Theatre), *Darling* (Hope Theatre), *Kicked in the Sh**ter* (Hope Theatre/ Theatre in The Mill, Bradford) and *Possum Trot* (Theatre at the Tabard).

Dani White | Stage Manager

Dani White is an Assistant Stage Manager who trained at Guildford School of Acting, University of Chichester and The BRIT School

Most Recently: Assistant Stage Manager Book Cover for *Aladdin* at Buxton Opera House. Other Theatre Credits include: Stage Crew at The Chichester Festival Theatre for T*he Unlikely Pilgrimage of Harold Fry, Marie and Rosetta, The Choir* and *Hamlet*. Assistant Stage Manager for *Taskmaster the Live Experience*, Deputy Stage Manager *Amelie* at The Rhoda Mcgaw, Stage Manager on Book *Persistent Shadows* at The Bridge House Theatre, Assistant Stage Manager *Born and Bread* Attenborough Arts Centre, Assistant Stage Manager *Candidates* at Rex Doyle Studio, Assistant Stage Manager *Twigs* at The Showroom Chichester, Deputy Stage Manager for *Buckets* at The Showroom Chichester, Assistant Stage Manager *Guinea Pigs* at The Showroom Chichester, Stage Management Placement on *The Spongebob Musical* UK and Ireland Tour. Assistant Stage Manager *2020 the Musical* Surrey Tour, Deputy Stage Manager *Taming of The Shrew* at The BRIT Theatre, Assistant Stage Manager *RENT* at The BRIT Theatre and Assistant Stage Manager *Dystopian Eye* at The Obie Theatre.

Adam Jeffery | Lighting Director

Adam is an award-nominated lighting designer and production manager from Essex. Recent work includes: *Jack and the Beanstalk* (Queens Theatre), *A Shoddy Christmas Carol* (Lichfield Garrick), *Three Little Pigs* (Unicorn & Chichester), *Speed* (Bush Theatre), *Animal Farm* (Bolton Octagon & UK Tour), *Statues* (Bush Theatre), *Foreverland* (Southwark Playhouse), *Playfight* (Summerhall Festival), *Communion* (Bush Theatre), *The End* (Bush Theatre), *My Father's Fable* (Bush Theatre), *The Bleeding Tree* (Southwark Playhouse), *Murder In The Dark* (UK Tour), *Elephant* (Bush Theatre), *After The Act* (New Diorama), *War & Culture* (New Diorama), *Under The Kundè Tree* (Southwark Playhouse), *Jekyll and Hyde* (Derby Theatre), *Project Dictator* (New Diorama & Edinburgh), *Everything Has Changed* (UK Tour & Edinburgh) and *Dorian* (Reading Rep).

Adam was nominated for The Stage Debut Awards for Best Designer 2025.

For Mum.

A new play by Ollie Maddigan

NOTES:

All characters are portrayed by THE OLIVE BOY in the moment.

All, expect the voice, which is a voice over.

CHARACTER:

THE OLIVE BOY is 15. He acts it.

A cheap looking chair sits in the middle of the stage.

As the lights dim a projection plays. One of a boy and his mother. A home video. A real video.

After 30 gentle seconds it cuts to black.

THE OLIVE BOY enters.

He wears a crinkled old school shirt and carries a backpack.

He sits down in his chair, ties his laces and then notices the audience.

THE OLIVE BOY: Well... I'm guessing you lot aren't gonna start?

> *He jumps out of his chair, bursting with energy as the lights change.*

I'm in the canteen. First day of school. First day of my new school! It's sunny outside...

Ya see, it's weird. You stand there with this gooey mac and cheese on your lunch tray, look around and begin to notice these groups, like these groups of kids. Students.

You see in my old school. The school before my big move to the city there wasn't any 'groups'.

We all kinda just

got

along.

I mean of course there was the odd ugly fat kid, that ya know, you legally have no option but to fucking torment! But like they don't really count, do they?

> *He laughs.*

This one time, there was this kid in school. Like this proper Fuckinnnnng

Uglllllllyyy

3

Unpopular kid, who only went and got himself caught holding his mum's hand in public.

For months after he couldn't come into school because we would all call him... wait for it.

MUMMY MUNCHER!

He laughs even more.

What a nonce.

But here, well here, like, it's different.

He looks around.

Okay right! So you have the snap streaks. The girls so hot and popular that the very sight of them just makes that dodgy P.E teacher kinda drizzle all in his pants.

Next up you've got the Nikes. The sporty kids, the ones that worship a basketball like it brought fucking life on to this planet.

Begins to gag.

And then last... and by far the least....... The sealers.....

The kids so ugly and unpopular that the very sight of them would make any VAGINAAAAA NO MATTER HOW BIG JUST SEALLLLLLLLLL UP! JUST—

He makes an impression on a sealing vagina. Continues to gag.

Oh, and there's this girl!

Like this GEEKY GIRL ! Yes exactly a GEEKY GIRL! Hair in ponytails, broken glasses taped on one side. Just carrying round this GIANT COCK-SHAPED PENCIL CASE. Ya know, just full to the brim of pens and pencils. The poundland multi pack…

SHE. IS.

DISGUSTING.

He pauses, notices someone.

I notice this cool, popular fella named JAKE walking through the canteen.

Oh, I can tell he's popular and cool from the way he's dressed. Hoodie over his shirt, joggers underneath his trousers. These cheap earphones tucked in his ears.

He slumps down in his chair and then notices me!

JAKE: Aight.

THE OLIVE BOY: *(To JAKE)* Aight.

Lights Flash.

They Stop.

(To the audience) I'm home. First day of school is over!

Dad's round his girlfriend's house. It's surprising… for a man with no hairline or really any purpose of existence he can go at it like a jackhammer.

There's not a lot of things that me and my father have in common. See, I'm 15 and personally happen to be the most exotic person I know. I'm like the perfect mix between cool mayo and GHOST PEPPER HOT SAUCE!

He slumps back in his chair.

Now I tend to spend the majority of my spare time texting these HOTTIES that are still just bloody begging for it from my old school. You know, nothing serious but it's good to still keep them on the hook, don't wanna burn any bridges too soon now, do I?

My Dad on the other hand is 40 years old and is more like a mix between…

He thinks.

BROWN SAUCE AND KETCHUP! Necessary but dull as shit!

He spends the majority of his spare time telling everyone, including me, that he's at the job centre.

"TRYING TO FIND A REASON TO GET UP IN THE MORNING!"

When in reality, we all know that he's still at home just jacking off to girls half his age on Pornhub...

Sparks up.

Which may I quickly just say is the most overrated porn site there is! I mean I'm 15 years old, I should know that if you want to have a proper amazing wank you've got to go in deep! You've never had a truly amazing bash till there's some virus on your laptop because you think you've just won a free iPhone 69.

Can't believe I fell for that...

My Mum is very different from my Dad. She would tell me these stories growing up.

Turns out I was born green due to a condition called 'meconium aspiration'. That's basically when the new-born baby inhales an-ta-nom-mic fluid whilst it's being birthed.

It's another way of saying I ate my own shit.

But my Mum, she would always say that the reason I was born green. Ya know, born like that. Is because I'm pure and sweet like an Olive!

Her little Olive Boy she would call me. Pure and Sweet!

Which is bullshit because Olives aren't sweet, they're bitter and way too salty and personally I hate them.

But she would always say things like this, little funny sayings she would often say to me! Like...

"I hope your sad days aren't that sad and that your happy days are really happy !"

I'd really like that about her. Made me happy.

Oh, she's dead now....

Jesus, no one's fault or anything just woke up one morning and BOOM there she was! Her body just stopped working. Like a car that is out of petrol.

Not a big deal or anything, life goes on, and anyway look at me now! NEW CITY!

NEW SCHOOL! NEW LIFE!

And the funeral was fun! Ya know got to see people that I hadn't seen in years, cousins and aunties and shit!

INTERESTING FACT! On the way to my Mum's funeral, my Mum's friend, like her best friend, well no, that's not true, but like she knew them, otherwise why would she be going to the funeral?

But anyway, she was in a car crash and just brutally died! I mean four people died in fact... So, like when you really think about it, like really think about it.

My Mum's funeral caused four other funerals, which is really poetic in the grand scheme of things.

He laughs again.

Peter was a mess.

Oh shit sorry, my Mum's fiancé, he looks a bit like a tall paedophilic slenderman but he is quite nice once you get to meet him.

He lives with his Mum now, I mean had no choice when my Mum died, how do I explain it?

He's like, he's like one of those, one of those comfort blanket people! Ya know the type of person to use someone as a comfort blanket? But when that blanket gets smelly or gets holes in, or in this case goes to bed one night and just doesn't wake up in the morning, kinda chucks it away and finds a new one! This one being his Mum.

I mean you can't really blame him, not everyone has the ability to move on with life and fucking smash it like I'm doing! Some people need peace with the fact that their only purpose on this planet is to eat, shit and die!

And anyway, he's much better than Dad!

Lights Flash.

They Stop.

A spotlight lands on THE OLIVE BOY.

THE OLIVE BOY: *(To 'THE VOICE')* Do ya not find this weird?

THE VOICE: In what way?

THE OLIVE BOY: The formalness of it all.

THE VOICE: What about this is formal?

THE OLIVE BOY: I mean you are wearing a suit.

THE VOICE: Would you prefer I wore something more casual?

THE OLIVE BOY: No... I wasn't saying that, I was just trying to say... Like who knew? I mean who does?... Like I just wasn't aware that therapists needed to, or tended to or just did... wear uniform. I mean what does it add to the job? You could surely do this in a onesie? I'm—... Have you got any water?

THE VOICE: Would you like some?

THE OLIVE BOY: Are there biscuits? I was told by someone round the corner that there would be biscuits. It's more or less the only reason I came, it is in fact the only reason I came.

THE VOICE: There are no biscuits.

THE OLIVE BOY: At all?

THE VOICE: At all.

THE OLIVE BOY: Ah, Okay...

THE VOICE: …

THE OLIVE BOY: Not even a fig? Ya know those figs ones, with that weird shit in the middle. You have to have one of those, no one eats those ones. It's not like I'm asking for a custard cream or a jaffa cake! Oh my God have you got jaffa cakes?!

THE VOICE: Shall we start?

THE OLIVE BOY: Start what?

THE VOICE: The practice.

THE OLIVE BOY: Ah yeah... Just to make sure there are no biscuits right?

THE VOICE: No.

THE OLIVE BOY: Okey dokey. Can I still have my water?

Lights Flash.

They Stop. Spotlight is gone.

(To the audience) It's been three weeks of school now.

We're watching this film in science class! I'm not paying attention to the film. It's crap and boring and presented by one of those men that talk from their nose.

He notices someone.

I see this girl from across the class. NOT THE GEEKY GIRL! This girl is.... Different!

We did catch eyes the other day...

But saying that anyone is bound to notice you after you stare at them for five minutes straight...

I'm not a creep! I'm not creepy to her! I'm not a stalker! Jesus Christ no!

Sinks down in shame.

Okay right, I did try to have a WANK to her instagram the other day but I thought it'd be too far to CUM! Like have some respect I told myself.

Have some decency. Jesus!

So I just finished myself off looking at my poster of Penny from The Big Bang Theory!

I like her hair! This girl, not Penny. She has this fringe but a sexy one. Tends to wear black but I've noticed that on Mondays she wears these pink little socks! I like that about her... I think it makes her stand out... look unique. Typically unique is just a kind way of describing someone who is weird or ugly. Like GEEKY GIRL.

But in this case. She's really unique. In a fit way.

Sometimes I do think about talking to her, this girl, the girl, THE SCIENCE GIRL.

But then I always think "no no no no." NO!

Don't actually go up to a cute girl, say hi and be kind. She'll just think ya gay!

Do the smart thing, the normal thing. Let her come to you! Play the waiting game! Just like fishing. Yes! Yes—speaking to girls is just like fishing! As long as your rod is out, someone is bound to put it in their mouth sooner or later!

He gets up from his seat.

It's a new day.

I'm walking home in the rain one day when I see JAKE! You know JAKE! Cool, popular, handsome JAKE! Just standing there under the bus stop!

Protecting himself from the hail.

I decide to talk to him…

(To JAKE) YO…

JAKE: Yo…

THE OLIVE BOY: Yoooooo

(To the audience) I decide to ask him if wants to come round my house! This week or next week I say! Not fussed I say! I am fussed I am very very fussed!

He turns to me again and replies with…

JAKE: EEEEEEERRRRRRRR… Will your Mum mind?

THE OLIVE BOY: NAAAAAAAA Bro.

Na she…

She ain't gonna…

mind.

(To the audience) We agree on a time and place and I get home and think to myself!

YES.

YES.

YES.

YES! This is doable, not easy but very fucking doable, if I play my cards right I could have JAKE! Cool, popular, handsome, talented JAKE as my friend! MY BEST FRIEND!

I plan this night out in my head, Mum would always say that a bad night is an unplanned night!

Music begins to play! Party lights shortly follow.

It will be me and JAKE! Right, so what do we do?! We drink, we drink our asses off, we drink like never beforeeeeeeee!

ALL THE STRONG SHIT!

BEER

CIDER

GINGER BEER!

We get absolutely shit faced!

(To JAKE) Hey JAKE! How ya doing?!

JAKE: Just amazing bro! Can I tell you something?

THE OLIVE BOY: Of course, JAKE you can tell me anything!

JAKE: You might be the coolest most legendary geezer I've ever met. I've just met you but for some reason I can just tell that you've defo got a PHAT cock.

THE OLIVE BOY: What can I say JAKE ? I am pretty cool!

THE OLIVE BOY begins to run around the stage. Taking us with him on this 'night out'.

(To the audience) We then go to a strip club where we shag two strippers each! That's four strippers shagged in total!

We then do this massive line of... of... of... KET!

Pretends to sniff 'Ket'

I mean I'm 15 years old and I've never done ket before! What is up with that?!

Leaving the club we get into a fight with some geezers for looking at us weird. One of them tries to get me with a left hook but little does he know that I spend at least 15 minutes a day watching karate tutorials on YouTube, I'm an un-official official black belt!

We hammer our fists into them! They just can't take it! I take on six by myself but Jake gets a bit carried away and kills two people! FUCK! No big deal! Nothing will ruin this for me!

We respectfully dispose of our victims bodies then run into school the next day where we tell everyone about our amazing night out!

The police let us off for being such—

FUCKING

LEGENDS

And SCIENCE GIRL runs into my arms where she instantly just—

He pretends to kiss SCIENCE GIRL

—falls in love with me.

Before you know it we are the yearbook for the cutest couple and every guy wants to be me and every girl wants to—

BE—

WITH—

ME.

He drops to the floor. Music and party lights stop. Back in the 'normal world'.

Saying that...He might just feel like staying in.

Lights Flash.

They Stop.

I'm back in class. Shitting science again! Writing these ideas for cool band names at the back of my book.

He notices someone.

I see the girl. The girl. THE SCIENCE GIRL looking at meeeee from across the class!

Play it cool I think to myself, stick to the plan! Let her come to me. The class is fairly empty.

Notices something.

Oh.

My.

God.

She.

Is.

Turning.

To.

Me.

THE SCIENCE GIRL: Hey.

THE OLIVE BOY: *(To THE SCIENCE GIRL)* Hi.

THE SCIENCE GIRL: What are you doing on Saturday?

He sparks up.

THE OLIVE BOY: *(To the audience)* When a girl asks you what you are doing on Saturday you always say you are free! Saturday is the perfect day for HAVING IT OFF!

THE SCIENCE GIRL: I'm having some mates round. Was wondering if you would like to... CUM.

THE OLIVE BOY: *(To THE SCIENCE GIRL)* One second...

THE OLIVE BOY runs to the corner of the stage.

Breathes.

(To the audience) YEEEEEEEEESSSSSSSSSSS.

YES!

YES!

YES!

YES!

YES!

> *He runs round the stage, collecting high fives from everyone in the front row!*

HIGH FIVE!

HIGH FIVE!

HIGH FIVE!

YESSSS!

Mates! MATES!

SCIENCE GIRL is having mates round her house! MATES! Me and SCIENCE GIRL are going to be mates!

And what do mates do? THEY MATE!

> *He sits back down.*

> *Breathes.*

> *Slumps into his chair.*

(To THE SCIENCE GIRL) Yeah, like, I might be free. I got to look in my diary and shit.

(To the audience) We exchange phone numbers and just like that, I've secured a party, a thing... A mate.

We do text now and again. Nothing serious, but whenever I post a picture up on Instagram she does tend to like it within the first six to seven hours…

(beat)

Dad doesn't really think I have mates. Well, no wonder why. He never saw me with any of my old friends.

Mainly because he was living here and I was up there with Mum. Only really ever saw him every couple of years. I mean the odd phone call every blue moon.

Him and Mum didn't really get along. I mean God knows why, I never asked her, never asked him, never plan to ask him. The least amount of conversation I can have with that man the better.

He's not cool and hip like Peter!

Peter would do anything for me! PETER THE PUSHOVER I would call him.

This one time and every word of this is true. Swear. Me and my mate forced him to buy us this packet of booze or I'd tell Mum how I caught him sneaking downstairs and three in the morning to spend £47 on Babestation phone calls.

Basically, he was all like "Errr, yeah guys sure guys, anything guys."

And we got our beers and got proper shit-faced in the park , a can and a half of Strongbow each. Whilst he got caught and had to pay this pretty hefty fine, almost got jail time for it. Was proper jokes.

(beat)

Never told Mum about the Babestation though.

He really would do anything for me. PETER THE PUSHOVER.

(beat)

Er, when... when Mum died. During the funeral, we had this book, like this gold, sparkling book. We got our, her... we got family and friends to write in it, you know, one last story. One final goodbye. Shit like that.

I was meant to write in the book.

Never did. Er, never had time, was always way too busy. And like when, whenever I did have time, I just couldn't think of what to write. Every word felt... Every word felt wrong. Nothing sat right on the paper.

He sits and thinks.

When I was eight, I was obsessed and I mean obsessed with Phantom of the Opera! I mean it's all I would ever go on about! One day Mum turns to me and says "let's go for a walk"... so we do.

Then that walk turns into a bus ride, that bus ride into a train ride and before you know it—

BOOM!

There I am. At the theatre! Watching Phantom of the Opera! Listening to the actors, dancing to the music!

The show ends and I'm just sat there like the eight-year-old kid who has just had the best prepubescent orgasm of his life! Just sitting crying like...

Pretends to cry.

Mum turns to me and says "wait here." So I do... Then three minutes later she comes back, followed with this built security guard with this kinda look of sympathy in his eyes. He looks at me and says...

BUILT SECURITY GUARD: You're a very lucky young man! You're getting to go backstage!

THE OLIVE BOY: (*To the audience)* Was, and I truly mean this, the best experience of my life! I got to meet the cast, the crew, get pictures with everyone!

Didn't find out until years later that she told them I had terminal cancer and wouldn't be 'around' to see the next tour.

Not very good, looking back on it. Not the most moral thing to do, quite fucked up actually!

But shit like that. Things that Mum would do for me, no matter how fucked up it was. Things that she would just to... to see me smile.

Those... Those are the things to write in that gold book. When I get around to doing so, that is...

THE OLIVE BOY stands up.

I'm on my way to the party! Carrying this bottle of cheap gin that I stole from my Dad.

He laughs.

Dickhead.

THE SCIENCE GIRL texts me. "What time are you getting here"

WHAT TIME AM I GOING TO GET THERE?! JESUS!

She is basically dripping for me at this point!

I see this bus drive by. It's got a poster for this movie on the side. 'Miss Peregrine's Home for Peculiar Children' it's called.

I reckon it's about the woman called Miss Peregrine and she has this home for peculiar childr— well, that's just obvious isn't it?

My Mum wanted to see that film. She was gonna take me to the cinema to see it. Never watched it in the end.

Never had time.

Still haven't seen it. Even after...

Yeah.

Just didn't think it would be fair. As Mum wanted to watch that film way more than me but died a week before it came out. So why would I get to watch it but not her, hey?!

Notices the audience.

Sorry… Just silly thoughts.

The closer I get to the party the more anxious I get. I did wash my cock in the sink before I left so I don't have smegma or 'cheesy balls' to worry about.

Before I know it BOOM there I am. Green door, big green door, I used to have a green door as well. See, soul mates.

I want to smoke a ciggy before I go in but I'm scared the SCIENCE GIRL won't wanna kiss me if I stink like a chimney.

Er... Sometimes I get these images, these pictures in my head. They never last too long but like sometimes they can... scare me.

But what I've learned to do is just steal one of Dad's cig's and then one puff and it's gone.

Dad does not know I'm going to this party. And I have no plans of him ever finding out. He's not cool and hip like Peter. No doubt he would just freak out!

And anyway...

How bad can parties be?

Party lights and music begin!

I'm at the party. Looking around. Trying to find THE SCIENCE GIRL but she's nowhere to be seen.

I'm standing in the corner and thinking how she must have lied to me. Because she said it was some mates, some mates round her house but there's no way she knows everyone here.

I mean the NIKES are here. The SNAP STREAKS are here.

Begins to gag.

Oh my God! Even the GEEKY GIRL is here! She's looking at me!

He moves around.

There's not even a snack bar, just a kitchen counter full to the brim of booze and a single bowl of OLIVES.

He sits down.

Before I know it, I find myself in this cult-like circle playing pass the joint with a bunch of stoned college boys.

I turn my head trying to find THE SCIENCE GIRL but she's still nowhere to be seen.

Gags again.

The GEEKY GIRL is still looking at me!

Gags even more dramatically.

I want to tell her to "FUCK OFF" and that "YOU ARE SO UGLY THAT NO ONE COULD EVER POSSIBLY LOVE YOU!"

But I'm scared that it might come across too harsh.

Notices something.

Before I know it, I look down and see that someone has handed this giant choodey-looking joint to me.

I smoke it!

Lights Flash.

They Stop.

He's high.

Very high.

Very fucking high.

Now

        there's

   five

        things

I

    learnt

        being

     that

        high!

He gets up from his seat.

Speaking directly to an audience member.

NUMBER ONE: No matter how hard you try... saliva... can never cure a dry mouth!

He speaks to someone else.

NUMBER TWO: How can a towel get dirty if when you come out of the shower, you are clean!

Someone else.

NUMBER THREE: Does Lighting Mcqueen buy health insurance or car insurance?

Someone else.

NUMBER FOUR: If you think about it. And I mean REALLY think about it. Technically, the brain named itself!

He moves back to his chair.

NUMBER FIVE: And by far the most important thing I've ever learnt in my life, Olives might in fact be the best bar snack of all time!

I mean I fucking hated these green balls of puke before tonight, but here I am just stuffing my face with the fuckers and I am loving it!

They're all looking at me like "look at this weirdo, cradling the bottle of gin in one hand and the bowl of olives in the other!"

But I do not give a shit! All I need are these little green pieces of heaven and I can conquer the world! GEEKY tries to take one off me and I'm almost forced to go GO KUNG FU PANDA on her ass!

Lights flash.

They stop.

Spotlight on THE OLIVE BOY.

THE VOICE: Have you ever done drugs?

THE OLIVE BOY : *(To THE VOICE)* Pft. No.

THE VOICE: It's important you be honest with me, there is no judging here.

THE OLIVE BOY: I am being honest.

THE VOICE: Tell me about the gold book. We spoke about it briefly last week.

THE OLIVE BOY: What about it?

THE VOICE: Why haven't you written in it?

THE OLIVE BOY: I... I don't have time.

THE VOICE : How long would it take?

THE OLIVE BOY: It's a big book. There's lot of pages.

THE VOICE: ...

THE OLIVE BOY: What?

THE VOICE: Are sure that there's not another reason?

THE OLIVE BOY: Like what?

THE VOICE: Some people are scared of accepting their grief.

THE OLIVE BOY: Why?

THE VOICE: Because it also means accepting that person isn't coming back.

THE OLIVE BOY: …

THE VOICE: Are you ready to accept that your Mum is not coming back?

THE OLIVE BOY: …

THE VOICE: Writing in that book would mean accepting that your Mum isn't coming back.

THE OLIVE BOY: …

Lights flash.

They stop.

We are back at the party.

(To the audience) I finally see THE SCIENCE GIRL. She's wearing this black silky dress, she looks lush! She walks up to me grabs my bottle of gin and just downs the fucker right there and then. The whole fucker.

THE SCIENCE GIRL grabs my hand as we enter her room. WE enter her room, just me and THE SCIENCE GIRL! We are alone… At last.

In her room it's green. Very green, she must like green. I see these chains on her desk and these baron pink socks lying around the room.

She's drunk. It's clear, she's swaying from side to side, dancing to the music in her head. She sits on her bed and turns to me.

THE SCIENCE GIRL: Come... Come... Come here!

THE OLIVE BOY: *(To the audience)* I do... I look into her eyes and see her hand land right on my leg.

Oh.

My.

God.

I sit and watch it, my eyes glued to her hand as it goes up.

And up.

And up.

And up.

And up.

And up.

And up.

And up.

And up.

And up.

And up.

AND UP!

And I just... I just stand up!

THE OLIVE BOY runs in the corner.

(To THE SCIENCE GIRL) You're drunk... Too drunk for anything like this I... I don't wanna take advantage of you or anything... I mean... I'm nice like that.

THE SCIENCE GIRL: Too drunk? Too drunk?! I'm so drunk that you could say or do anything right now and by tomorrow I would have forgotten all about it! So come on...

THE OLIVE BOY : *(To the audience)* I stand there. Listening to what she said. Replaying the words over and over again in my head.

(To THE SCIENCE GIRL) I could say or do anything right now? And in the morning you would have forgotten everything? Anything?

THE SCIENCE GIRL: An.. ey.. thing.

He thinks.

Unsure what to do.

THE OLIVE BOY stands up.

Runs to the corner of the stage.

THE OLIVE BOY: *(To THE SCIENCE GIRL)* I'VE NEVER KISSED ANYONE BEFORE!

I've never had sex or a blowjob or anything! I mean the only girl's hand I've ever held in public was my Mum's and some people in my old school saw me and called me MUMMY MUNCHER!

I couldn't go to school for months!

And, well, like I was only holding her hand because I knew, like I knew that any day... any day I could wake up and see wouldn't be around anymore. I was only trying to treasure my time with her! Well, she's dead now so who's laughing hey! Well, they are... They're still laughing...

I just thought.. I just thought that if I... That if I made you think, like made you feel like I wasn't such a 'virgin'... like such a fucking loser ! That you would maybe, like just maybe want to be my...

I don't want to have sex with you. I mean we can. It would be nice, like I've never had sex before I mean JESUS I'VE NEVER EVEN SEEN BOOBS BEFORE! I would love to see your boobs, like I'm sure you have amazing boobs, but mainly, like truthfully I would just like to you know…

Treat you well. Take you out, go for walks and shit. Buy you stuff I can't afford and go to fancy restaurants. I mean we would have to do a runner, like I can't afford to pay but I'd still very much like to take you. Just… Just spend time…

Make your sad days not that sad and your happy days very happy.

Begins to cry.

Because ever since I moved here, like to the big city, ever since I moved here I have not felt happy.

And sometimes, like not all the time, but sometimes I'm walking down the street and I get these images, like these fucking things or my Mum, like MY MUM just lying there, just lying there. THERE!

THERE! JUST LIKE WHEN I FOUND HER DEAD! DEAD!

DEAD! DEAD!

DEAD!

AND I FEEL LIKE I HAVE ALL THIS LOVE TO GIVE AND JUST NO ONE TO GIVE IT TO! SO I ACT LIKE I'M THIS LEGEND, THE PLAYER, THIS FUCKING GEEZER! WHEN THE TRUTH IS I'M JUST…

I… I er, I don't know. I don't know who I am. Or, what I want. Or, anything.

But I do know that… I don't want this. That I really don't like this. I don't like anything about this. Not one bit.

(To the audience) She stands up, begins to kinda drunkenly walk to me. Swaying like a leaf in the wind.

I open out my arms, expecting a hug, a "thank you for all you have shared today." She looks into my eyes and then finally speaks.

THE SCIENCE GIRL: So what…You've never kissed anyone?

THE OLIVE BOY: *(To the audience)* I stand there, silent, ashamed, fucking embarrassed!

Begins to gag. A lot.

I go to speak but before I can this tsunami of half-digested OLIVES just spur out of my mouth!

Half land on me, half land on her!

THE SCIENCE GIRL: *(Screaming)* Oh. My. God!

THE OLIVE BOY: *(To the audience)* In a fairly reasonable response she then begins to throw up on me, before you know it we are just two fountains of sick just pouring against each other!

I get my things.

I leave.

I FUCKING HATE OLIVES!

He leaves.

I get home, walk through the door and Dad's just standing there.

Fucking pissed! He looks me up and down. Smell's the drink on my breath. See's the sick on my clothes.

THE DAD: Where were you? It's half three in the morning.

THE OLIVE BOY: *(To the audience)* I think of something funny to say, maybe try and take away the tension a little bit.

(To THE DAD) Disneyland, heard it's nice this time of year.

THE DAD: Look, if you're gonna go to a party just tell—

THE OLIVE BOY: *(To THE DAD)* Oh, who says I was at a party?

(To the audience) He rubs his hands on his face and laughs.

THE DAD: I think you were at a party because it's half three in the morning and you've just walked in with vomit all over your clothes…

THE OLIVE BOY: *(To THE DAD)* Ahah! Yes Dad but not my vomit!

THE DAD: Oh, so who's vomit is it?

THE OLIVE BOY: This girl from the party.

THE DAD: Ah, so you were at a party!

THE OLIVE BOY: Oh fuck no! Ah, I mean maybe.. Okay YES! YES DAD I WAS AT A PARTY BECAUSE I'M 15 YEARS OLD AND THAT'S WHAT YOU DO!

THE DAD: Have you been drinking?

THE OLIVE BOY: Oh why are you pretending to give a shit?!

THE DAD: Because you are a child. Because you are my son!

THE OLIVE BOY: Oh fuck off am I a child?! Fuck off am I your son! If I'm a child, if I am your son then where were you?! WHERE WERE YOU?! Where were you when you fucked off to the big city and left me to look after Mum. To watch her get sick, to see her go, to find her dead in a pile of her own fucking vomit! WHERE WERE YOU! If you want me to be a child so badly then when have you robbed my fucking childhood from me! Left me! LEFT ME WITH MUM! No Dad! I'm not a child, I have spent my entire life being more a man that you can ever be! Do you have any fucking idea of what it is like to be told that your one responsibility in life is to keep someone alive and then they die whilst you sleep! Do you even the slightest fucking clue?! So, do not stand there and act like I'm a child, when the truth is, is that I am more of a man that you will ever fucking be!

THE DAD: I know, just, calm down!

THE OLIVE BOY: Don't tell me what to do, you prick!

THE DAD: I wish you would just listen to me for one sec—

THE OLIVE BOY: AND I WISH YOU HAD DIED INSTEAD!

(To the audience) I don't know why I said that. I guess I did at the time. I tried to take it back. I promise. I did try...

He just stared at me with a tear in his eye then walked away...

(To THE DAD) Dad... Dad... Dad, can you just wait...

(To himself) Fuck.

FUCK!

(To the audience) Oh.. THE SCIENCE GIRL does not forget by the way. No. She runs into school the next day and tells everyone. They all laugh at me...

The 'snap scores'. The 'nikes'.

Even JAKE.

MUM would have let me go to the party. I think to myself. Mum wouldn't have minded that I had sick on my jumper. Mum is so much better than Dad. Than pissing old Dad!

I just can't be here right now I think. I just can't be here! I just want to go home. I just really need to go home.

Lights flash.

So that's what I did! One bus back home, one train and one bus back home! Back to my real home, my home with PETER and Mum! MY REAL HOME! Just away from Dad and this girl and this school and everything! BACK HOME!

Lights stop flashing.

He stands centre stage, staring outwards.

I've ran away. I'm standing outside my house—looking at my green door. It's different to what I remember it looking like. My house. My old house. My green door. It's weird I used to look at that green door and think, "home, food, comfort, shelter."

But as I stand here and look at it all I can see is my Mum getting carried out in a body bag.

Just like the bins on a Tuesday.

I see my old neighbours looking at me from across the street. "Ain't that the kid who use to live here?"

"Ain't that kid whose Mum died"

Because that is all I am... I am just the kid with the dead Mum and it's not fair...

PETER doesn't live far from here I think to myself. I'll go see PETER.

I just really need a comfort blanket.

One bus, the X9, looks like shit and smells even worse but it's getting me to where I need to be.

Did you know that Peter lives in a house that was originally built for one of Henry the Eighth's wives.

She never needed to use it... I get off the bus.

I walk though his patio and knock on the door.

I hate waiting for the door to answer. I'm clenching my fists. I've been crying. I don't want him to know I've been crying. I don't want him to know I've run away, I'll make something else up.

The last time PETER saw me was at the funeral, I didn't even cry then. I did a speech and all a proper good one, I could be Shakespeare.

I see him in the reflection of the window. He's halfway through shaving. Half foam-half beard.

He looks like shit.

He sees me and instantly just ducks. Like he's hiding from me.

I stand there just knocking and knocking, shouting and shouting!

"PETER open up!"

"PETER it's me"

"I've seen you PETER"

"Why won't you let me in?"

"PETER" … "PETER it's me".

Nothing.

I have a sandwich in my bag. B.L.T. Marks and Spencer's, fucking expensive!

After 15 minutes of waiting by the door, this ancient woman slides the door halfway open. Half her 90-year-old face popping out behind the chain.

THE OLD LADY: He doesn't want to see you.

THE OLIVE BOY: *(To the audience)* PETER's Mum. She has to be lying I think. PETER loves me. PETER would do anything for me! PETER THE PUSH OVER!

I go to walk in but, before I can, she slams the door on my foot! I manage to hold it open, before I know it we are tugging with the door—

Left
Right
Left
Right
Backwards
Forwards
Backwards
Forwards

FUCK ME WHY IS SHE SO STRONG ?!

Then out of nowhere this chain just goes fucking flying though the air as a door handle breaks.

I stand there, I feel my eyes watering. My lip's trembling.

(To THE OLD LADY) Why doesn't Peter want to see me?"

(To the audience) I say.

And I will never forget what happened next, what happens next, he come's running downstairs fucking fumming, runs straight passed his poor old Mum and looks me dead in the eyes.

Goes to speak, goes to say something, anything! But just…

Stands there.

Freezes.

Grabs me and holds me in his arms.

I don't speak. I don't say anything, I just stand still. Allowing him to hold me.

Then after two minutes, he lets go, turns around and slowly begins to walk back into his house.

But just before he can. Just before he does, just before I see PETER for the last time, the last ever time I ever have and ever will see PETER he does say one thing to me. One final thing to me. The last thing PETER will ever say to me.

PETER THE PUSHOVER: I'm sorry boy… You just look too much like her.

THE OLIVE BOY: *(To the audience)* And just like that. No more PETER THE PUSHOVER.

Just like Mum… gone.

You think about going home. Saying sorry to Dad.

Buying THE SCIENCE GIRL new clothes. NEVER HAVING OLIVES AGAIN.

He remembers something.

Lights change, we are in the past.

On the way home from the party, before I ran away, I just laid down in this park. Found this park and just laid there.

Olives and vomit lingering on my clothes. Seething in the cotton. I laid there and I just thought—

WHAT IS THE POINT OF THIS MUM? WHY AM I TRYING TO GET BETTER, TO BE HAPPY!

Because everyone I know is happy! But everyone I know who is happy, is happy because they have a Mum, or a good Dad or friends or something that I don't have!

And I am never going to get you back Mum, so why would I ever think that I'm going to get my happiness back?

He sees something.

And I must have been a little drunk, or high or something because the next thing I see is this figure, this figure in the distance walking towards me.

I see this figure and I just think 'Oh. My. God. It's my Mum, it's my Mum she's back.'

He begins to run.

So the next thing I know I am just running to her, running as fast as I can! 'Mum I have missed you' I think. 'Mum I am so glad you are back'. "Mummy—

He stops.

I stop when I see who it is.

(To the person) Why are you following me?

THE PERSON: Because you looked sad.

THE OLIVE BOY: I'm not.

(To the audience) I lie.

It's GEEKY GIRL, she followed me home from the party.

GEEKY GIRL: I heard what you said.

THE OLIVE BOY: *(To GEEKY GIRL)* What?

GEEKY GIRL: In the room, with that girl. I heard everything. I wasn't spying. I just heard.

THE OLIVE BOY :If you tell a soul, I swear to god I will—

GEEKY GIRL: I'll kiss you.

THE OLIVE BOY: What?

GEEKY GIRL: I'll kiss you… It's easy. I've done it loads of times.

THE OLIVE BOY: *(To the audience)* I stand there, she stands there. She moves forward. I move forward. She puts her hand on my face and I put mine on hers.

Our lips touch. We are kissing.

They Kiss.

She pulls away.

(To GEEKY GIRL) Is everything Okay?

GEEKY GIRL: Yeah… you just really taste of sick.

THE OLIVE BOY: My bad.

(To the audience) I had my first kiss with GEEKY GIRL!

Lights change.

We are in the present.

On the way home… home, not home but… Dad's. On the way back to Dad's I just sat on the train.

Looking out the window, seeing the trees go past, the clouds passing by.

Goodbye, green door.

Goodbye, PETER.

Goodbye, Mum.

I get home. I get back to dads. I knock on the door, I have keys, I can get in… But I knock.

He answers almost immediately.

I stand there, looking at him. Not talking. Nor does he. We just spend a minute looking into each other's eyes, and then finally when I'm ready…

I…

I…

I'm…

(To THE DAD) I'M SORRY I HATE YOU! I'm so sorry I hate you! But, I just really hate you and I can't… I can't… I can't help but hate you because whenever, I mean Dad. You don't know what it's… how it's… I mean Jesus, Dad, I know it's not your fault but I just can't help but hate you! And fuck me, I have tried not to hate you but I really really hate you! Because… Because whenever I look at you, I mean whenever I see you or hear you voice or even say "Dad", I just get reminded that you're not… you're just not… and will never be… you'll never be … her. You're not Mum.

I hate you Dad and I will always hate you because you are not my Mum, and you will never be my Mum. I'm sorry.

(To the audience) He stands there. Not speaking. I see the same tear roll down his face. He sits down and then finally speaks.

THE DAD: I'm not your Mum, boy. You're right. I'm not your Mum and I will never be your… I was never… I haven't been… But I am… I'm not your Mum and I will never be your Mum and I know you'll always hate me for that. But maybe… maybe one day… You could love me for being your Dad… Because I am your Dad… and I will always be your Dad.

Lights flash.

Lights stop.

The same spotlight as before lands on THE OLIVE BOY.

THE OLIVE BOY: Where's Dad?

THE VOICE: He's waiting outside.

THE OLIVE BOY : Can I see him?

THE VOICE: Can I ask you a question?

THE OLIVE BOY: Okay...

THE VOICE: What do you see when you think of her?

THE OLIVE BOY: What?

THE VOICE: When you think of your Mum, what do you see?

THE OLIVE BOY: …

THE VOICE: Love? Happiness? Sadness?

THE OLIVE BOY: Yeah happiness, I feel happiness.

THE VOICE: What's your real answer ?

THE OLIVE BOY: …

THE VOICE: What do you see when you think of your Mum?

He cries into his lap.

THE OLIVE BOY: Olives. I see olives. She would always call me her little Olive Boy.

Oh God.

And then when she died, like when she died and I, I found her.

Her hands.

Her feet.

Her face.

Her skin.

My Mum's skin….it was all green and purple.

Everywhere.

Just like an…

Olive.

THE VOICE: That's all we have time for today.

THE OLIVE BOY: Oh. Great place to end.

THE VOICE: I can book you in again next week if you want. Only if you want?

THE OLIVE BOY: Yes please, that would be nice. Bring biscuits next time !

The spotlight goes.

We are in the theatre.

THE OLIVE BOY looks around.

He goes to leave, but something stops him. He sits back down. He takes a deep breath and takes out a book from his bag.

It's gold.

It's the gold book.

The real gold book.

He shares the writings inside.

The things that real people, real friends and real loved ones said about her.

Their goodbyes.

He doesn't read them all. Nor does he read read the entire message. Just the parts that he wishes to.

Every night is different…

'Dear Charlie.' They all say Dear Charlie.

'Dear Charlie'

'Dear wonderful Charlie'

'Dear our Charlie'

'Dear the best Charlie'

Dear Sweet wonderful Charllie

you made me a better person for knowing you. I love you so much I miss you more than words can say. we were so blessed to know you and feel your friendship. IU nev forget what you said.

Pippa

xyyy

Charlie

With love, I have the fondest memory of Christmas at The Bell with you, Wayne & Henry, that was a hard time & you lightened my day after the loss of someone close. you were a light in many lives & will continue to be so. you are already missed by so many.   Laura xxx

Charlie I first met you when you appeared in a play with Matthew at Lewisham College and you kissed in the play. Later Matthew introduced me to you the rest is history, Oliver came along and made your family complete. When you moved away from London I understood but missed Ollie a lot, especially him growing up. Everything you did was for the best for your children and for that I have absolute respect. You have done a wonderful job as a Mum. Love you Charlie.

Betty xx.

To our Charlie,

Goodbye Gorgeous Lady, you have be an inspiration to us all,

Thankyou.

Aunty Christine xxx and uncle Foster

To Charlie,

I'll love and miss you forever, and I promi
till we have to m

He gets out a pen from his bag.

(To MUM) Dear Mum!

Music Begins to swiftly play.

Dear Mum, I love you. I have always loved and I will always love you. Thank you for raising me, for nurturing me, for holding me and loving me.

Not one day goes past where I do not think of you, where I do not miss you and I am not afraid to say it anymore. I'd hold your hand everyday if I could. I'm not afraid to be the kid with the dead Mum because I would have rather had you as my Mum for 14 years than anyone else's for 60.

This grief that I carry isn't a burden. It's just the price to pay for having someone as amazing as you in my life, for loving you so much. It's the price for love. And it's worth it.

I will get better, I will get better because at the end of the day life is so much more than a bowl of olives. It's love and loss and pain and happiness and grief and anger and hope and lust and sorrow and laughter and joy and everything! Life is everything!

And life without you, although very hard, if I try hard, I can make it everything.

Sleep well. I miss you.

Sincerely, your Olive boy.

THE OLIVE BOY places the book down. He goes to leave.

But before he can, projections play. Home videos of THE OLIVE BOY and Mum.

THE OLIVE BOY growing up with her by his side.

It's how the show opens but yet, there's more. Real videos, real memories. Projecting all across the stage.

The music sores in the background.

He sits there, watching.

Until the tears begin to dry. And a smile takes their place.

BLACKOUT.

THE END.

Charlotte Bella Comber
1979-2016

ALSO AVAILABLE FROM SALAMANDER STREET

All Salamander Street plays can be bought in bulk at a discount for performance or study. Contact info@salamanderstreet.com to enquire about performance licenses.

EAT THE RICH (but maybe not me mates x)
by Jade Franks
ISBN: 9781068233449

Witty, provocative and utterly current—a bold exploration of class, privilege and power from one of the UK's most exciting new playwrights.

COWBOYS AND LESBIANS
by Billie Esplen
ISBN: 9781914228902

A funny, heartfelt coming-of-age story about friendship, sexuality and finding your place in the world.

CARA AND KELLY ARE BEST FRIENDS
FOREVER FOR LIFE by Mojola Akinyemi
ISBN: 9781068233418

A darkly comic two-hander that exposes the nastiest sides of teenage girlhood.

CHICKEN BURGER N CHIPS
by Corey Bovell
ISBN: 9781913630447

A vivid portrait of South London youth, told through sharp dialogue, big laughs and moments of raw emotion.

POSSUM TROT by Kathy Rucker
ISBN: 9781068233432

Possum Trot, Nebraska, is on the brink of disappearing. Can the owner of its one diner keep the soul of her town alive?